The Ashbourne Circle

John and Ann Gilman

CHURNET VALLEY BOOKS
© John and Ann Gilman and Churnet Valley Books 2003
ISBN 1 897949 94 4
Printed and Bound by Bookcraft, Midsomer Norton

Disregarded today as old gate-posts or cattle scratchers, these isolated stones once marked our ways and paths across the landscape.

CONTENTS

The Maps

It was ever our intention that readers would go out into the locality and find this amazing trail for themselves. Driving it is reasonably simple but to appreciate it fully you will need to make a number of stops and follow the line as it weaves through a village or makes over an important crossroads. To this end we have included a series of simple maps covering some of the villages and towns the line passes through.

The maps only provide the perimeter as a dotted line. A closer and more concentrated survey on the ground will reveal many minor twists and turns on a local level. It would prove a lengthy research exercise to create a detailed map of any village location with all its associated lines. Even a hundred metres of lane can contain a wealth of information. Our hope is that the reader will want to take the basics here and follow them up to a more detailed picture of their own locality.

Obviously with sixty-eight miles, it would prove impossible to do the entire ellipse in a single day. We took nine hours just to photograph it, stopping only briefly. We suggest exploring it as the four quarters outlined in the text. This will enable readers to stop and appreciate some of the more interesting features of the pattern and even dowse for themselves.

Photography by John & Ann Gilman

ST. OSWALD'S CHURCH
ASHBOURNE

DRIVING
THE ASHBOURNE
CIRCLE

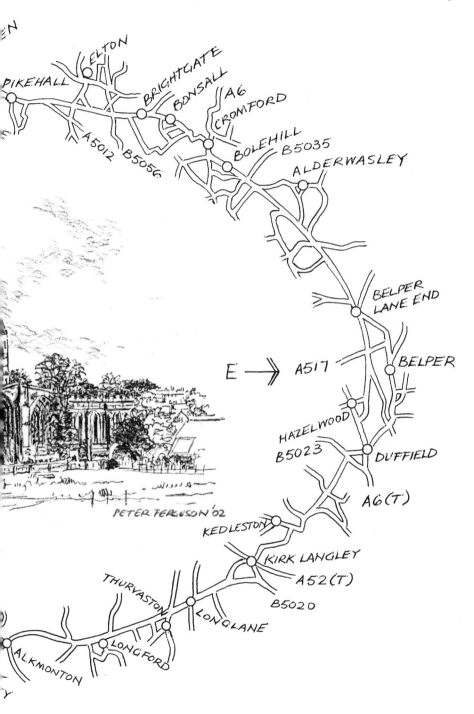

PETER FERGUSON '02

Hidden Circle John Gilman

1. The Beginning

Fundamentally, this is a book about a remarkable dowsing exercise; not dowsing for water but dowsing for a distant water influence that is as powerful today as it was when first discovered by our Bronze Age forefathers.

Although between us we have been dowsing for many decades, it was not by intentional dowsing that indications of this amazing discovery first came to light. That happened over ten years ago when I regularly drove home at the end of the day to Ipstones along the A523 from Leek. Upon turning at Bottomhouse, I consistently experienced a lowered level of tension. It took years to notice that it happened a few hundred yards along the Ipstones road and resulted in an easing of the day's pressures. At first I put it down to the fact that I was now almost home and could look forward to a break from the day's worries but somehow it seemed more than that. It appeared that this particular section of road had a form of influence upon me and this was beneficial.

Being a dowser meant that this should, one day, be tested out to see whether or not there was anything apparent at this point. So one afternoon I stopped, took out my dowsing rod and paced the road up and down, back and forth, asking if there were any significant energies that underpinned this strange revelation. There were! A strong line swept along the course of the road from Bottomhouse towards Ipstones. On one side of it there appeared to be an area of calm and power and on the other, nothing. It seemed to take the near-side edge of the road as it approached Blakemere Pond, then left the road and passed through the pond itself before continuing into the fields on the left.

That initial dowsing established that we were on the edge

of a pattern or pool of energy and that the line established the perimeter, boundary or limit of that energy. Just how big the area was or how significant, we had no idea. That it was significant was almost palpable. Those first dowsing probes all agreed on this.

The obvious thing to do was to undertake some map-dowsing and to discover just how far this edge or perimeter fence extended. Was it a small, local pool of energy? Was there a source? Were earth energy lines that dowsers are familiar with involved? What was found was almost beyond comprehension but the physical signs implanted on the present landscape confirmed we had stumbled upon a vast, ancient and extraordinary wheel of power.

Blakemere on the Bottomhouse to Ipstones road.

2. What is dowsing?

Before we look at the geographical or archaeological aspects of dowsing perhaps it would be helpful to look at dowsing as a broader concept. A much under-used facility of the human body that has enabled us as a species to discover more about our environment than is immediately obvious at a cursory inspection. Put simply, dowsing is an awareness of things not easily apparent in the first instance.

The village dowser didn't need to dig a dozen trial bore holes on a property before sinking an expensive well and was equally confident where to strike an adit into a plentiful deposit of iron ore. Every community had its dowser, wiseman, conjurer, or diviner and the skills were passed down the generations. Although only recorded on paper from the 1600s, dowsers have been active for thousands of years in this country and across the world. Their techniques are similar wherever vestiges remain, even in isolated and remote areas around the world and we have discovered from Europe, Australia, West Africa and India that, although dressed in a different costume, the basics are the same. Today, dowsing is as much a part of everyday life as it ever was, from aerial dowsing, map dowsing, mineral surveys to complementary therapies and even sexing chickens.

It is highly likely that, in common with the animal creation, all humans are gifted with the latent ability to dowse. (Although it has to be said that a few of us find it almost impossible!) We discover it in all nationalities and at all times in human history. It has still to be fully understood and whereas in Victorian times it was surmised to be a response to an electro-magnetic impulse or wave, today it has been established that it is most likely to be an inherited response to particle energy; a bit like a built-in metal detector although even the most sophisticated metal detectors are not able to match the abilities of a skilled dowser. However, just as a detector is able to discriminate between metals and detect minute electrical differences between disturbed levels of subsoil, so the dowser can discover and outline ancient foundations, building plots and long vanished sites, circles and dwellings and even reveal the long established patterns of human movement around abandoned village sites.

For example, one of the exciting things that we do on visiting monastic and ecclesiastical ruins is to find the site of the altar and where the priest used to stand to say Mass. Sometimes the site is marked but more often than not it is just rough turf.

How does the dowser do this? We have heard it described as an active interrogation or a focussed questioning, a disciplined exercise of mind. The dowser learns to adopt a single-minded concentration on the goal and poses questions. Some dowsers carry a reminder or 'witness' of what they are seeking but this is merely an aid and not really necessary; the whole facility is in the mind. Answers are experienced in a bodily reflex that can be a flick of the wrist, a muscular twitch or even a blink. Sometimes it is no more than a mental assertion or confirmation that is felt. The reactions are legion and each dowser learns to develop his or her own highly tuned routine. A skilled dowser learns to recognise every minute response and instinctively knows just what each means.

No two dowsers work in quite the same way. There are those who swear by the hazel twig while others use a hefty pair of metal rods. My own preference is for a single small metal rod set in bearings for a swift response whilst my wife is better with a pendulum. Some use a tiny instrument held within the hand while others use a bobber, a coiled spring, a piece of whalebone, a strip of plastic or even a section cut from a polyurethane pipe. In the end it is the body that responds and the instrument only enlarges that response. In some cases, even the instrument can become redundant and the dowser relies on a bodily reflex alone.

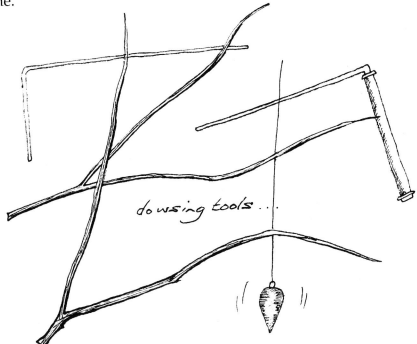

dowsing tools ...

The oldest dowsing tool on record is Roman. Called the lituus, it was made of wood and twisted into a spiral at one end. The earliest illustration of one, found on pottery, dates from c. 4000 BC and Romulus was supposed to have used one in laying out the foundations of the city of Rome but perhaps this is only saying that ancient Rome was laid out on earth energy lines.

A commonly held belief is that it is the instrument itself that reacts and it is the rod or wand that moves and if you watch a country dowser with a hazel wand you might believe this is so as the twig is drawn down so powerfully. A number of folk who begin dowsing are often zealous to acquire rods of a particular kind but it doesn't make the slightest difference really. If you believe that a particular rod will work better for you, then it probably will. We can assure you however that it is the reactive muscular twitch that sets the rod in motion and not any inherent power that the rod might have. Put briefly, it is the individual dowser who sets the agenda, arranges the scales and levels of reaction and makes the rules. It is the dowser who says, "When my foot crosses this point, the rod will move." It is the dowser who ascertains the depth and flow of an underground stream by his own agreed method and for him that will work. How well the dowser achieves is up to his or her discipline, approach and individual reactions.

Both Annie and I are dowsers of many years and in many fields of interest. We are both adept at using a variety of instruments from rods, twigs, pendulums and even hands alone but both of us understanding the basic concepts of dowsing, namely that it is a highly tuned mental discipline requiring concentration, sensitivity and common sense. There are no substitutes in dowsing for practice and fine-tuning and it is these qualities that allow the dowser to advance in understanding and expertise. There are, of course, barriers to clear-headed dowsing and the most common is the ease with which the mind can overrule or ameliorate results by wilful thinking or a logicality based on previously accepted facts such as, "There can't possibly be water here. It's solid granite!" Another delicate area is the problem of dowsing matters relating to self and here self-interest can block a clear-sighted objectivity.

Of course there are the tempting 'impossibilities' that the novice dowser may be inclined to think they have overcome such as trying to dowse future outcomes. Strong likelihoods are easy but can provide no more than intuitive guesses given a reasonable input in the first place. The dowser soon finds what can be done and what is accurate and relevant as he checks out the results. Digging for indicated water or searching for that lost watch will prove individual talents or the lack of them.

It is not surprising that the sceptic scoffs at much that the dowser takes for granted for such skills as map dowsing or dowsing at a distance stretch the credulity. Nevertheless, map dowsing is a much-used tool of the dowser saving him a great deal of time wandering about in the field looking for a needle in a haystack. So much easier to map-dowse first and ascertain just where in the field he should be looking in the first place. Let the scientists worry about the physics or biology of the art, the fact that it works is the important thing for the practitioner who has work to do.

This, of course, brings us to the point where we become cognizant of the two major schools of thought that would discredit dowsing. First, the scientist who would hang his hat on Newtonian physics and look for the universe working as a clock, ticking away to a set of immutable rules. Because dowsing did not fit in precisely with the known laws of electro-magnetism it was suspect. Quantum physics is now beginning to knock holes in this once firmly held view, as it appears that the rules do not always apply.

The second is the body of fundamentalists and sectarians of the Christian church who would banish the skill as a demonic or occult practice allied to the Devil. These base their assertions on a body of theological literature from the distant past and are mainly to be found where a literalist approach has set up a series of protective prohibitions. It was fine for the doctors and elders of the church to investigate dowsing and to use it (the greatest body of literature concerning dowsing emerged from the French Roman Catholic Church) but it was forbidden to the common folk for fear they might fall into mischief.

Accordingly in this Country the dowsing art was left much alone by the Church of England for centuries and treated with the same sort of suspicion and horror as the planchette or the ouija-board. Despite this it persisted in the village communities, among miners and engineers, and in the practice of holistic country medicine. Strangely, it remained strong in a field allied to Christendom, that of the medieval cathedral and church builders. Here, as any competent dowser can discover for himself, the whole building concept is based on underlying energy and water lines, each distinctly marked for those who have eyes to see. All pre-Reformation churches comply and are laid out on specific lines with doorways, windows and internal steps conforming to the pattern extant within the site. As many of these structures were erected on older sites of socio-religious significance it becomes plain that the builders of ancient monuments, temples and circles were aware of the energies underpinning them. In other words, a dowser laid them out in the first instance and the building or circle was a response to what was discerned underneath.

In the same way, dowsing is able today to discover the layout of ancient vanished buildings as quickly and accurately as those folk using modern instruments of radar, sonar and electronic pulses. It is worth mentioning at this point that it is not the dowser's desire to dig up vast stretches of the countryside like some popular TV archaeological curiosity digs. Quite simply, there is no need. The dowser knows what is there. He knows whether the barrow, dolmen or low contains a burial and what implements are buried therein. He knows how deep and whether or not the incumbent has been disturbed. It is not necessary to remove those who have been laid to rest with ceremony, nor is it proper to drag important leaders and holy men and women from their appointed places on the hills. In fact it is a violation of our ancestors' intentions, beliefs and wishes. Most lows, if intact, (and not smashed by such as Bateman and his modern equivalents) still contain a measure of their innate energy and the person of importance so interred complements this. We know of several such that still generate useful power and set as they are on the hill-tops give a potent meaning to the biblical line: "I will lift up mine eyes unto the hills, from whence cometh my help."

Today, dowsing is gaining in popular acceptance as more and more try it for themselves. As I have suggested above, there are few that cannot master it, as the gift it obviously is for both animals and humans. It was likely to have been born of necessity, a highly tuned facility of awareness that allowed many corners to be cut. In fact it could be called an evolutionary device that supported life itself. Watch the sheep as they knock the modern walls down or damage the hedges to follow that known and easy track. See the example of the medieval farmer who placed his gateways strategically to utilise the natural forces within the landscape. He was not blessed with abundant labour and so had to use the land as sensibly as possible; no rebuilding walls every season, just get the gates in the right

The remains of the chapel of St. Barr, Barra, Western Isles.

place first. Watch where animals give birth, go when frightened or retire to die. They will all be special places that are supportive. When seriously ill, I used a prominent local line as a prop that was most effective. Why we have lost so much of this once valuable knowledge is likely to be down to the priests who wanted social control of the parish and consequently preached against such superstitions.

Nowadays most dowsers are aware of the huge scope and breadth of the art. Some will find their forte in dowsing to help and heal other humans. Some will use their skill in helping animals. Some will specialise in archaeological dowsing, tracking those buildings that have long vanished and the walls that no longer stand. Others are able to diagnose problems within structures, outlining cracks, faults and weaknesses. Still others locate ghosts and spirits or are able to find missing people. The uses are legion and, once started, the dowser will find himself or herself drawn to the field in which his greatest potential can be developed.

We have found it fascinating to discover the dimensions of small Celtic chapels planted within the landscape according to the ancient rules and now are either totally within the confines of an overlying Christian church or halfway in and halfway out of one. Usually the significant east/west line passes up the centre of the older building but not always up the chancel of the overlying church. That the lines were the basis of the site in the first place is often supported by other evidence in terms of standing stones, markers or the remains of ancient groves. It was not always the case that the line followed an exact east/west conformity but it certainly followed the earth energy line. So much of what we have as part of our regular current landscape has been influenced in the past by the response to underlying energies. In fact we have discovered that everything from the shape of hilltops, the line of woodlands, wells, banks, prominent springs, most settlements, and the planning of a large number of major communications in terms of roads, fords and bridges are all predetermined by a regard to ancient indicators. Dowsing makes us realise that there is a great deal more to the accepted structure of our lives and that most of what we accept as regular features of the landscape are, in fact, responses to the earth upon which we scratch and dig.

It is probably true to say that all dowsing is a response to or interaction with the earth upon which we live. Together with the animal creation, we are of the earth and therefore best adapted to work with it. That the Bronze and Iron Age Celts were aware of that which lay beneath their feet is all too obvious to the dowser who finds so many clues, signs and markers left behind. There is nothing new out there and when we discover just how extensive their view was, our respect is huge.

The Meeting of the Lines — John Oilman...

Old springs and wells were often later capped with a pump.
Springs on earth energy lines were especially important.

Ipstones.

3. Marks on the Landscape

Nowadays, most dowsers are aware that ancient building sites and other social and religious structures leave strong indications of their one time presence. From old tracks and vanished villages that might occasionally appear on aerial photographs after drought, ancient henges, circles, barrows or lows, to lost meres, mines and tunnels. If it is out there or has been out there, it is accessible to the dowser. On many occasions as the dowser discovers and plots a strong line across the landscape he finds that it has been previously marked and if it is a specially beneficial one, for instance a line connected with healing or power, then it has markers set out for others to see.

Perhaps the most common mark is the stone, erected at a particularly relevant site. One of the most common of these was the mark(et) stone or cross set up at a crossroads or junction of two lines conducive to social interaction. Almost all villages had one at some time although there are examples like Windyway Mark on Ipstones Edge (replaced in 1882 when the earlier stone was damaged) that were used for trading as well as a waymark but were not in a village setting. These focal points became the trading posts and early markets and the stone often developed into a 'butter' cross or 'yarn' market. Most of these were later Christianised by the addition of a cross on the top and there remain many fine examples like Bonsall's. Dowse them and you will find that they stand at an intersection of lines. There are two such on the Leekbrook to Basford road. One at the intersection of the Cheddleton

market cross...

The Butter Cross.   Basford.

Heath/Finney Lane crossing (currently hiding in a holly thicket under a beech tree) and the other on the intersection of the footpath that goes from Bridge Cliffe Farm to Lowerhouse Farm. This section of back lane and footpath was once part of the major north/south highway that comes across Gun Hill from Macclesfield. It is an extremely ancient route and still has five remaining accessible cross sites or marks upon it within a few miles of Leek.

Decorated stones are rarer and many that were incised with pagan motifs were damaged by Christian zeal. Others, as I have said, were Christianised by the addition of a cross on the top or the cutting of a cross into the shaft. Stones lucky enough to have a pagan cross already upon them escaped. Although just outside our area of interest, in Leek churchyard there are two pre-conquest marks one of which bears a knotted pattern reminiscent of the Celtic 'head' motif. Both have suffered damage and both have been moved from their original sites. There is no agreement on their age but the yard itself is an extremely significant one and the site covers the intersection of two strong lines. Verbal tradition points to the existence of a stone circle at this point and, of course, there is the popular vantage point for the famous double sunset, which until very recently was visible for a few days each year around the summer solstice.

Ridgeways, highways, Roman roads, Saxon trails and tracks, mostly conform to pre-existing Celtic and British routes across the land. For the Celts, the high moorland tracks, or the moor-ridge routes (Morridge) followed and intersected with powerfully indicated lines. They were easily dowsable and the tribal elders would therefore have the key to travel over vast distances. Local and inter-tribal lines were marked as well so that the uninformed traveller could find his way. Look for some of these on the Mermaid to Warslow road. These early roads, mainly on high ground, are not to be confused with the 'ley

Cleulow Cross.

Leek Cross.

Lows...

lines' of Alfred Watkins which are a different thing altogether. (Although marked in a similar way, they are the straight tracks of an even earlier age used for travel and the trade in necessities at a stage before most settlements were conceived.)

Most of our old roads are pre-Roman although the Romans used huge stretches of them and developed the network further. The reason why so many of them are called Roman is simply because they established them in stone and imprinted their identity upon them. There are quite a few Roman sections of road locally, some now under major modern roads and some still running alongside country hedges and banks out in the fields. The older ridgeways are easier to find as they are still up there on the skyline. All local Celtic and Roman roads are dowsable and follow important energy lines.

Some of these ancient highways and salt tracks have since become footpaths. This is easy to see if you look at an Ordnance Survey map of the area and follow, for example, the old highway from Macclesfield through Lowerhouse, Hollinset, Cleulow, Wincle, Bearda, Gun End, Gun Hill, Fould, Abbey

sight . stone ...

Green, Leek, Sheephouse, Basford. The way is marked 'all the way' by stones, gates and stiles, some with their massive marks still in place despite the destruction of the hedges and wall around them. Where these paths crossed fields established on the instructions of the Inclosures Act, farmers came under pressure to remove marks that were now in the way. Many were dragged away

and broken up. Many minor circles were also lost in this way. On the southern slopes of Morridge there are the remains of two small circles cleared and broken and the residue pushed to the side of the fields. One was close to a powerful circular line and was obviously connected in the ancient scheme of things. The great delight for the dowser is when he finds a massive standing stile still astride a powerful route as intended. It is a miracle that so many remain.

Sight stone ...

Is there anything so ordinary as a gateway? You might think that a gateway is just a gateway but you would be wrong. If the gateway is recent, then it is probably just to gain access to a piece of land, a house or drive. However if the gateway is an older one, then it is likely to be where it is for a reason. Animals, like humans, are great natural dowsers and work better with nature than against it. For animals, and here we refer to domestic farm animals such as sheep, cows and horses, it is far easier to be

Windyway Mark.   Ipstones Edge.

way stone ...

drawn along a favourable line whilst grazing or moving from pasture to pasture than not. Try moving a flock of sheep single-handed from one field to another without a couple of dogs! The trick was to place the gates on the natural lines so that the sheep would follow them without hassle. All old farm gates are so placed. Natural lines pass through them and encourage rather than hinder the creatures that would enter. Then, of course you will remember that the original meaning of the word gate meant road or track and not an entry leading to it.

The same is true for humans. Humans, that is, who built their houses before the Reformation. The skill lingered on in the countryside for longer but by Georgian times most houses were not conforming to the ancient principles of allowing a blue or white line to enter the front door. These beneficial lines brought healing into the house and encouraged harmony, co-operation and dialogue. Nowadays it is all too common to find houses sitting on angry lines that are having a marked adverse effect on the inhabitants. Conditions are exacerbated and often rheumatism and arthritis, headaches and minor respiratory problems are encouraged. Sometimes all that is necessary is to move the bed and favourite chair off the offending line but far better to have dowsed the place first!

sight stone ..

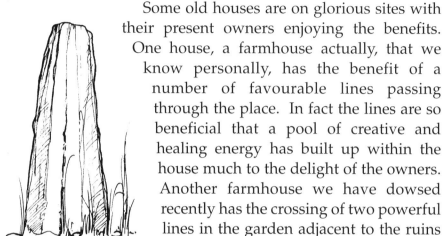

gate - stones ...

Some old houses are on glorious sites with their present owners enjoying the benefits. One house, a farmhouse actually, that we know personally, has the benefit of a number of favourable lines passing through the place. In fact the lines are so beneficial that a pool of creative and healing energy has built up within the house much to the delight of the owners. Another farmhouse we have dowsed recently has the crossing of two powerful lines in the garden adjacent to the ruins of an older house. This is a powerhouse of positive energy and any human or animal that sits there cannot fail to notice the difference. A good clue for the dowser is to watch where the dog selects to lie down when he has the choice. He is not going to lie on a bad line.

Some of the very old dwellings may well have marks to indicate where the lines enter. Churches very often do and if you look under the east window you may be lucky and find a smallish prominent stone in the footings of the wall. Sometimes it is an incised cut that marks where the line passes.

So far we have been looking at some of the ways in which a line is marked as it passes through a region. There are, of course, many other indications that a line is present. All these lines represent entirely natural features of the landscape and are the result of geological and geophysical factors. Perhaps you will remember doing an experiment in school where the science teacher scattered a handful of iron filings on to a sheet of paper. He then placed a powerful magnet under the sheet and, hey presto, the iron filings started to form patterns and lines. Now imagine a stretch of countryside where under a prominent hill lies a few million tons of iron ore. A few miles to the south there is another range of hills, this time enclosing a further few

A violated low.   Pealow, Alstonefield.

million tons of ore. It is not difficult to conclude that there will be lines of force connecting the two. If the local polarities are opposed, then there may well be some turning of the lines in the locality. This is simplistic as there are any number of forces active under any part of the country. The earth's crust is moving and there are significant tensions and enormous pressures involved, as the occasional earthquake clearly shows.

Dowsing lines of earth energy then may be little more than a sensitivity to various kinds of geological excitement or

Low Plantation.   Alstonefield.

Waterfall Low.

stress. Just why some of these expressions of excitement are
beneficial to us earth dwellers have yet to be identified but the
benefits and penalties have been recognised for thousands of
years.

We have not really begun at the beginning for if we were
to set out all the responses of the animal kingdom to earth
energies, we should begin with animal tracks as they also strive
to follow identifiable lines. In fact some major routes and
motorways started out as just that and if traced back in history,

Low on Grindon Moor.

include animal tracks, paths, lanes and minor roads on the same line. It is fascinating to discover a footpath, a Roman road and a modern bridge all on the same ancient line.

All along these lines are points of importance. Some occur when the line is crossed by other significant lines thus generating focal points of varied character. (The folklore and history of crossroads supports this.) The line is also affected by local water, by rivers, but especially by springs. The blind spring particularly has a marked effect or reaction causing local anomalies. It is here that one can often find the socio-religious sites of the distant past. Here are the lows, the mounds, the circles and the meres. Here are the important burials and the holy places. Sometimes the mounds and lows show themselves and it is the practised eye that can recognise them dotted along the evening skyline but more than often they have been ploughed up, knocked down or destroyed. For many circles, there are avenues outlining the ceremonial walkways that set the feet on the right path for the meetings. On Dartmoor, Exmoor and across the Pennines as well as in Wales and Cumbria, many of these remain but in most cases the stones that marked these avenues have been moved or cleared.

Most small Celtic chapels overlaid earlier sites and they in turn were overlaid by Saxon and then Norman churches. These in turn were rebuilt often in the 14th century when the great perpendicular churches were constructed. If there remained any stones or markers from the earlier periods then it was a matter of luck or intent. At Bakewell there are a considerable number of stone artefacts from the later Anglo-Saxon period, and at Wirksworth the whole circle is still visible in the form of the round churchyard with some of the stones broken and incorporated into the building.

Sometimes, as at Pilton in Devon, the pattern of seating within the older part of the building echoes a small circle and instructions not to intrude on this space have been handed down through the centuries from churchwarden to churchwarden. A local dowser has identified the centre as the site of an ancient oak. A marker stone still plots the approach to the site. In many places, it is a story that has been handed down how the foundations of the first church were mysteriously moved in the night thus indicating just where the church ought to be built. Minehead in Somerset and Kingsland in Herefordshire are two such but this story can be found right across the country.

There are many extant ancient national structures like Arbor Low in Derbyshire that have not been overlaid and although damaged and pillaged, still lie open to all comers in much the same format as built. There is still some controversy as to whether the stones were ever erect on this site but that is really not important. Much energy still remains and the male and female entrances are still identifiable. Dowsing a stone circle can be a very interesting experience depending on what you are looking for or open to. Perhaps you are asking, "Why here?" "Is there a centre?" "Is there a healing spot?" "Is there a joining spot?" "Do the stones have special characteristics?" "Is

Vandalised Circle.   Below Morridge.

there a ceremonial or altar stone?" "What energies are still here?" "Are there any outer circles of influence?" "Any burials?" "Any signposts, avenues, boundaries, links?"

Here we cannot help but mention again that the dowser is able to gain all the information he seeks without ever disturbing the ground. We know of several local burials within lows that have escaped the Victorian zeal for looting. In one in particular, a tall male elder lies together with his sons. He still wears his torque and there are items of gold and bronze alongside him. The bronze is in the shape of a sword but much damaged by long years in the earth. Whereas, as dowsers we are happy to work alongside the professional archaeologist, we are not interested in destroying or uprooting original sites as has recently become very popular with certain television programme producers. Personally we deplore such ham-fisted activities in which a sensitive site is hacked at in a few hectic days and bodies, once layed with respect, are shipped all over the country to learn what a competent dowser could tell them in an afternoon's quiet walk across the countryside. It is a pity that the stories of guardians and curses cannot do their job in our age

Brownlow.   Near Warslow.

Bonsall Cross.

as in past ages and these sites kept sacred. Having said that, we have just been dowsing over an important local site with intact burials and where there are still reports of ghosts and strange lion-like animals in the vicinity.

Another ancient feature of the landscape is the bank. Sometimes associated with a ditch and often built up with huge stones, they marked important boundaries, at first tribal and then parish and political. Many of these, if not most, are drawn along important lines of energy. This was originally so that they could be easily identified by the tribal elders or Druids but later the locations of divisional banks and important boundaries were annually walked or 'beaten' to establish their positions. 'Beating the bounds' is still a feature of country life in many parishes and there are a number of local boundary stones and ditches that remain from pre-Roman times. Sometimes the names of farms and dwellings echo these sites like Standing Stones Farm at Bottomhouse on the A523 where there remains a boundary stone erect.

Remains of a circle below Flash.

A spring from a limestone crag.

4. The Centre

This book is about the impact of a powerful spring sited at a particularly 'holy' spot in what is now rural Derbyshire, as seen by our remote ancestors in this region.

Once the Bronze and Iron Age families had made significant inroads into the river valleys and forested lowlands below them, a new network of local trackways interlinked with the long established ridge-ways. The well published freedoms of sea, river and track were honoured by the Celts and they were travellers and traders from the first. Although there were well-drawn tribal territories across Britain, interaction was encouraged. Travel for learning, cultural pursuits and trade was common. As the forests shrank, many villages and townships sprang up especially in places of socio-religious importance. Strategic sites, easily defensible positions, river crossings and important sources of good clean drinking water attracted dwellings where life might be easier. With the establishment of lowland farming and the certainty of trade, communications became established first for decades and then for centuries. It is fascinating just how many routes today follow roads and tracks established first in Celtic times.

As regards a settled, creative, intelligent native population, this region was old long before the Romans came here. Above all, it was wealthy. There were extensive local minerals. There was a European-wide trade in the best wool and woollen cloth to be found anywhere in the world. As regards scholarship, the Druidic tradition encouraged learning and the preservation of huge bodies of knowledge from astronomy to herbal medicine, poetry, history, philosophy and languages. They were widely travelled and artefacts from all over the known world have been found locally. When the Romans arrived in Britain it was remarked that the Druids were the arbiters of local boundary disputes and only they had the living proof of where the 'lines' were sited.

One such busy crossroads was Ashbourne in Derbyshire. Positioned on a bountiful spring of excellent water the site offered every kind of pasture from water meadows to sheltered slopes. A copious supply of pure water was equal to that of an easily defensible site - one was hardly an advantage without the other.

From a Celtic viewpoint Ashbourne had the benefit of an exceptional spring which rose from marshy ground alongside the River Schoo or Henmore. This particular spring had the advantage of rising at the crossing of two powerful lines meeting at right angles. That this was a recognised religious site is underlined by the presence of the parish church of St. Oswald built right over the spring. The lines are to be found today crossing under the spire on the 'crossing' of nave and transepts. (This is where the original 'crossing' was but today's dowser will discover that the point has moved about a foot or so to the left of centre. The east/west line is a powerful one consisting of a 'white' centre band with 'blue' on either side. The north/south line is a wide band of 'blue'. Both are consistent with healing. Today's dowser will also note that the east/west line tracks up the chancel a little to the left of centre, orientated 070 degrees East.)

It is well known that the Celts valued and revered sites where such springs issued forth. Most were protected with the heads of significant leaders buried close by. All were marked by stones or by groups of stones, and the wells that drew the water were marked as sacred. There are still legends extant about the association of heads with wells and churches. One such is the well of St. Decuman at Watchet in Somerset, hard by the church of that name. The story tells how St. Decuman was praying by the side of the well when his head was struck off by a local. He calmly washed it at the well and replaced it before continuing in prayer. What this is telling us is that there was a connection

St. Decuman's church and well. Watchet, Somerset.

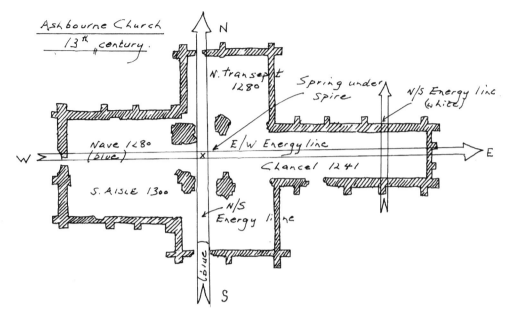

Ashbourne Church
13th century.

N

N. transept
1280

Spring under
Spire

N/S Energy line
(white)

Nave 1280
(blue)

W

E/W Energy line

Chancel 1241

S. AISLE 1300

N/S
Energy line

X

E

(blue)

S

between early Celtic Christianity and the cult of head worship at certain important sites. This story also successfully indicates that the well was an ancient one associated with a severed head, and was re-dedicated as Christian at the time of Decuman's missionary expeditions across the Bristol Channel in the 6th century. (We don't seem to have altered this tradition much as the majority of Britain's churches are still decorated with heads.)

Ashbourne's spring is a plentiful and powerful one and there are indications that it finds its way to the surface at more than one outlet. Emerging from an aquifer at a depth of some thirty metres, the water is of great quality. It was one of the first of Britain's bottled waters (1926) and remains a favourite despite the many other varieties now on the market. Within living memory there was a well close to the church that provided drinkable and healing waters. That there are still other minor branches of the main stream is indicated by the boggy nature of the ground to the west of the church despite the fact that several boreholes have been introduced at source.

A modern analysis of this water reveals that it is

St. Oswald's church. Ashbourne.

particularly high in calcium with 100 mg per litre. This is twenty per cent of the recommended daily adult intake. It is also low in both sodium and nitrates.

Dowsing indicates that at a depth of some 2,250 metres there is another large stream of water that follows the course of the east/west line down the chancel of the church. This is very powerful indeed. There is no indication of where it is going but it is likely to have derived from the limestone of the Peak. The depth is no surprise as Buxton's famous supply comes from a depth of 1,500 metres and there are recognised water sources beneath continental limestone that are deeper.

This spring and underground river must have become apparent to the Druidic dowsers who first crossed and re-crossed their tribal territory. It is well known that the Celtic tribes throughout Europe were in constant contact not only trading but also sharing knowledge. Much Druidic training was centred in Britain from all across Europe and a well site of this magnitude would have been a matter of considerable tribal pride and therefore become well known. However, unlike

Marshy ground to the west of Ashbourne church.

Bath's 'aqua Sulis' and Buxton's 'aquae Arnemetiae', this spring remained signposted for Celtic use only.

As far as we know there are no remaining early Celtic artefacts in the vicinity of the church as at other Derbyshire sites such as Bakewell. If there are stones at Ashbourne, then they have probably been encased within the present fabric of the church building. (There are remains of some Saxon work in the north transept.) With the departure of the Romans, the Saxons gained control of this region and it became part of Mercia with its capital at Repton. The area was likely to have been Christianised by the middle of the 7th century, probably through the leadership of four missionary priests, Cedd, Adda, Betti and Diuma.

It is highly feasible that the original wooden church building and the subsequent stone structures were built over the well site and the water piped or led to a collection point close by. This arrangement is common throughout the land and many present churches have, or had, water emerging from spouts and wells adjacent to the main building. (Leek is one such where water and lines join to create an important site. The remains of the well can be seen at the south-western corner of the churchyard.)

That the builders of the present church at Ashbourne (consecrated in 1241) were aware of the spring that underpinned their church is indicated by the fact that the distance from the spring to the west door equals the depth of the aquifer below the crossing. All other arms of the spring are marked by steps in the chancel, the final step to the east indicating not only another blind spring but also another significant line crossing the building.

Another interesting thing to note is the shape of the churchyard. Just as Wirksworth's churchyard echoes its past, so Ashbourne's churchyard forms an ellipse slightly flattened from north to south. The building does not sit in the centre but hugs the lines about the spring. If anything, the shape of the original churchyard, not the Victorian extension, apes the wider circle set into the landscape around it and could well have been an indicator for those who had eyes to see.

So we have a pre-Christian Celtic site, important for its water, its powerful lines and its association with healing. Just how important and how powerful this site was, is indicated by the remains of a perimeter trackway or path that marked the outer limits of the spring's influence. A dowser is easily able to 'find' a source of water such as this and further to mark the pulses of energy that occur at the surface at intervals from the centre. These are not ripples but signals from the upward thrust of the combined energies of the spring and river. We are not dealing with a small or even an average spring here but a giant of significant proportions capable of use today by a large factory and for a bottled spring water plant. Currently, several boreholes are in daily use.

Within the boundaries of this spring system there lies an area influenced by it and distinguishable from the region beyond. Its perimeter was marked and formed a track-way which, in turn, has developed into a chain of pathways and roads extending many miles around the area. A look at the map will discover that the age of the roads involved ranges from Celtic ridge-ways to Roman roads, from animal tracks, farm tracks and minor roads, to fast major highways. This venerable pathway traverses fields, gardens, rivers and field boundaries but always it is followable and distinct in a particular way. It is still easily dowsable as any competent dowser will be able to verify. It sweeps around the countryside in a flattened ellipse with a Roman road to the south and a decayed limestone reef to the north. Some parts of the route link villages, as they must have done thousands of years ago, and some parts trek between ancient barrows or lows, and barrow-meres or ponds. Some parts of the route have been duplicated alongside the original track leaving the ruins of the way to hug the present road amid brambles and scrub. Sometimes the route sweeps off 'cross-country' only to emerge in line some hundreds of yards further on.

Barrow - mere ...

At first we thought that little might remain in terms of evidence for this discovery but our fears were proved groundless as we walked the route. To follow it was an adventure and a revelation. It became quite obvious that our distant forefathers had seen this rough circle and marked it out on the ground.

In a nutshell, what we have re-discovered is probably one of the largest ancient circles in the United Kingdom. It may well

Old pack-horse track.   Near Brighton, Hartington.

Sheen Hill near Longnor. Our Bronze and Iron Age forefathers lived in these places
before moving down into the wooded valleys.

be part of a greater tribal or regional picture, similar to the Glastonbury Zodiac, but at this stage of our investigations it is sufficiently exciting to recognise we are at the centre of a very old pattern discovered by our Celtic ancestors that still generates the same energies for those who are able to appreciate them.

For the Celts, there was a healthy respect for the earth and what it had to tell them. They respected their environment as a living entity, as a deity and established a symbiotic relationship with it. They buried their dead at important key points and revered their supplies of God-given water. They were aware of what the earth could offer in terms of healing and support. It may well be the case that today we are bombarded so much with radio emissions that we cannot receive the gentler vibrations from the planet beneath our feet but the Celts had only this steady input to guide their thinking. It was natural for them to believe that the earth was making some form of contact with them especially at the points where energy lines and springs made themselves felt. Where the earth 'bled', as at the issue of ironstone springs such as that at Glastonbury, then this was extremely significant.

Let us now travel together around the Ashbourne Circle as we have come to call it. It is not really a circle, more an ellipse but as you follow it on the ground, it sweeps around its centre at roughly the same distance from Ashbourne, reminding us that we are within the holy limits of that once great eruption of water. It is not a ley line as all these are straight lines that emerged in the late Neolithic period. It is very probably late Bronze or Iron Age and represents a departure from *The Old Straight Track* of Alfred Watkins and the 'tracklines' of Guy Underwood as described in *The Pattern of the Past*. As such, although I suspect not unique, it is an ancient perimeter of holy ground and probably the first of these natural occurrences to be rediscovered.

5. The Circle

Before we begin a circumnavigation of some sixty-eight miles around this powerful area it is perhaps pertinent to mention a few relevant facts. As humans we are great destroyers, shifters and movers of things. If there appears the slightest reason for demolishing or removing a prominent landmark, then it will be effected. Thus we have lost thousands of glorious buildings, hundreds of magnificent churches, hundreds of ancient monuments, circles and mounds and a countless number of smaller marks. The question must always be, 'Is this stone genuine and is it in the right place?'

As it turns out, some stones are original and genuine but no longer in the right place and some stones are in the right place but are replacements for the original. Along with the Druids, who were the original judges as to whether a particular stone had been moved from its intended site, the dowser must ascertain whether or not any particular mark is in its original place or moved to facilitate road widening or building. As we travel around the route we shall find examples of all permutations possible. There are still some fine original marks to be seen on our journey but few are exactly where they should be. The ones that are, can usually be found at the side of roads that see only the occasional car, and more hay wagons than lorries dedicated to logistics.

The next thing to be aware of is the way in which the original trackway has been modified or nudged to allow for widening, cutting corners, avoiding obstacles or creating easier crossings over rivers and streams. Modern bridges do not always follow the original ford lines and railway engineers often rebuilt hundreds of yards of roadway to effect a route over or under the tracks. As traffic has increased so almost every

St. Oswald's church.   Ashbourne.

road in the country has been modified in some way or another. This means that our perimeter line may pass down the left of a particular road for some distance and then be found on the right or in the ditch as the route progresses. This can be fun when dowsing from a motor vehicle and the line suddenly shifts across the road to take up its course on the other side of the road!

Having said this, it is absolutely amazing just how many marks on the landscape still exist despite the passage of thousands of years. It has proved a delight to discover, for instance, that a large square stone weighing approximately two tons is still sited at the point where an ancient footpath meets with the road at exactly the spot where the perimeter line passes through. Although it is today almost buried in the hedge, it is still doing the job it was designed for, namely to mark a way.

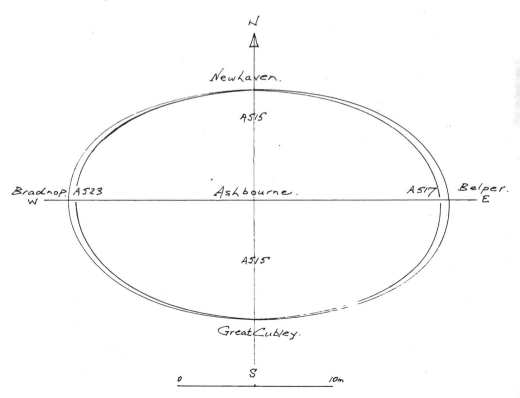

We have said that the area enclosed by this line is an ellipse. However, it is not perfect in a mathematical sense. It wobbles and it wriggles. There are some quite sharp corners at a very local level but the overall broad picture is that of an ellipse. It is possible to drive around the circle quite close to the original pattern, sometimes leaving the line only to pick it up a little further along the road.

The area we shall be travelling comprises a journey around the Staffordshire and Derbyshire countryside. It crosses the Churnet and the Dove (both retaining their Celtic names to this day), as well as several other minor rivers and streams. There are still important crossroads at the north, south, east and west of it, and it is roughly bisected in both directions by major roads. At the northern end we find Newhaven on the A515. At the south, Great Cubley on the A515. To the westward there is Froghall on the A52 and to the east, Crossroads Farm on the A517 just short of Belper.

A word here about ways and a definition that might show the reader the nature of that complex network of routes we have inherited across our land. Sir Edward Coke (Institutes, Vol. 1. 1639) sets them out as follows:

"There be three kinde of wayes, whereof you shall read in our ancient Bookes. First a foot way, which is called iter, quod es jus eundi vel ambulandi hominis, (a way that is a right of going on the part of a man) and this was the first way. The seconde is a foot way and a horse way, which is called actus ab agendo and this vulgarly is called a packe and prime way because it is both a foot way, which was the first or prime way, and a packe or drift way also. The third is via or aditus, which containe the other two, and also a cart way &c. for this is jus eundi, vehendi, vehiculum et jumentum ducendi, and this is twofold, viz. Regia via, the King's High way for all men et communis strata, belonging to a Citie or Towne, or between neighbours and neighbours."

Way mark.

Way mark and pointer.

Anciently, the most prolific and most common was the footway and the footpath network. This tended to be quite distinct from the other two systems and often ran parallel to them. Very often, when the other two became impassable due to being churned up in winter,

stile stones ...

this footpath network was the only safe way to travel. It is important to understand that the present footpath network shown on the OS maps and often found with difficulty on the ground is only a very poor shadow of what once existed across our country. A close study of 17th and 18th century inclosure plans and estate maps (such as those from Keddleston Hall) will clearly show that many of the little bits of pathway that serve

Way mark and squeezer.

today to cut corners were once a part of a continuous system. What we lost at that time was nearly thirty per cent of the whole and what we are losing today through lack of use, disease on farms and strong local land ownership is likely to be another thirty per cent. Just about every ancient footpath lies on a track-line or energy line thus adding that small consistent ingredient of support that made all the difference to our ancestors.

The loss of field paths through inclosure was already being bitterly lamented in 1827 when William Hone penned a long letter on the subject in his *Every-Day Book*. If we return to the medieval period, the only heavy vehicles in regular use were the distinctive county variations of the hay wagon and these would be found mainly on the limited tracks from the open field systems toward villages and townships. Long overland tracks for the transportation of salt and pack goods supported pack-horses only and anyone who wished to travel long distances overland had to rely on the horse or shanks's pony. It was to be the middle of the

Way mark.   Heathcote.

17th century before the first coaches began to establish regular routes although there are records of convoys of heavy wagons making itineraries across the land in the previous century.

It was Ogilby's *Brittania* of 1675 that attempted to set out the first definitive outline of our national communications network. This has been called the father of the modern road atlas but for our purposes it is perhaps better seen as the base line from which we can see all modern developments in logistics. We need to understand that, at that time, apart from the streets of towns and the backs of bridges, there were no properly maintained surfaces throughout the land. The surface depended on the traffic and how much use the way suffered. Too much and the way decayed into a sea of mud. Too little and the edges grew together.

Ways were first closely defined or confined between established walls and hedges with the inclosures and plantations of the 16th century and culminated with the wholesale parochial inclosures of the 18th and 19th centuries. Once so defined, the responsibility for establishing a more durable surface was put upon individual parishes, and the beginnings of passable roads and lanes grew out of drifts, bridle-ways and prominent footpaths.

The idea of making the traveller pay for the upkeep of ways was no new concept but it was to be the early 18th century before turnpike trusts made themselves felt. It was the turnpiking system however that brought about a revolution in national travel with its legislated mile-stones or posts. (See the one on Morridge near the cross-roads for Onecote.)

The reason why we have so many variations in width among our roads is interesting. Our Roman roads, according to Marcus Terrentius Varro, were set at eight feet for a via (highway) and four feet for the actus (driftway). The Highways Act of 1772 laid down that cartways leading to a town should be twenty feet wide and every horseway or draftway should be set

Morridge.

at eight feet wide. Widening has been going on ever since leading to the interesting fact that some old bridges have round arches of one period on one side, and pointed arches of another period, on the other. (Cromford Bridge and Hanging Bridge, Ashbourne, where the new bridge has been set on top of the old.) There are so many examples of widening, cutting corners, rebridging and altering roads and highways, it is foolish to cite more examples here. Suffice it to say that dowsing can establish the original line and its width.

Despite the fact that our route will tread on Bronze and Iron Age, pre-Roman, Roman, Saxon, Early English, Medieval, turnpike and modern roadways, it will be the iter, quod es jus eundi vel ambulandi hominis that underpins them all. From Celtic times the iter was sacred and, with the rights of passage on sea and rivers, open to all.

This is why it is important to record and keep what is a part of our very early heritage and not allow it to decay or fall out of use. It is our right to quest and dowse our country and to keep alive the ancient ways of our ancestors.

Hanging Bridge. Mayfield.

18th century turnpike stone on the Winster to Pikehall road below Elton.

Sandy Lane.

6. Bottomhouse to Great Cubley

We begin our tour of this ancient route at the Green Man at Bottomhouse, on the A523 Leek to Ashbourne road. Public house names certainly have a lot to offer and perhaps it is no surprise to find a 'Green Man' on the western side of the circle. We also have an ancient parish boundary stone within a hundred yards of the line that suggests that it once might have been a mark on the line. There are also a number of large stones to be found in the adjacent field. There could well have been some form of monument at this point. The farm that presides over the crossroads is called Standing Stones Farm although this has only been a major crossroads in recent history. Just about in line with the boundary stone is an earlier track running parallel with the new one but behind the farm. Both cross our line within a hundred yards.

Proceeding southwards towards Ipstones on the 1769 Turnpike, the line follows the road until it reaches the small rush-filled pond at Blakemere. Here there is a lay-by and slight mound. The line passes through the mere as might be expected as many of these isolated ponds are, in fact, marks in their own right. Called barrow-meres, they indicate sites of special significance such as the confluence of energy lines, the passage of leys and the presence of blind and active springs underpinning major pathways and tracks. Often in association with lows or barrows, they have persisted through history despite losing much of their original size. There are a number within the circle and at least three actually on the line. We shall meet another Blakemere further along our journey. Both have farms associated with them and the name has been retained in both cases.

The perimeter here leaves the road and passes into the field on the left. The reason is that the present roadway was here diverted to allow for the construction of a railway bridge. The earlier road, narrower than the present one, ran alongside about thirty metres from the highway. As might be expected, it passes through a gateway and strikes out up the hill on a converging path towards the crossroads at Ipstones Edge. You can clearly see the depression in the field as the old road passes up the hill, along current animal tracks, through a narrow modern copse on land belonging to Sextons Farm and on to join the present road at the crossroads. Here, the line rejoins the Bottomhouse to Froghall road and can be found pretty well in the centre of the tarmac. This is another public house site (for a long time the Red Lion) although the house is now privately owned.

At this point the line crosses an important ancient ridgeway from Sharpecliffe Rocks to Gander Well, Ramshorn. The crossroads here is extremely old and is likely to be of Iron Age construction. The sceptic may indicate that this road is first and foremost, a turnpike but even turnpikes were mostly consolidated from older routes.

We follow the main road down into Ipstones and the line stays with the road until just past an ancient well, capped in Victorian times with a pump, when it takes a diversion along the older lane behind the smithy and the redundant Methodist chapel. This is currently a very narrow lane with older stone buildings along one side and a high grit-stone wall on the other. The later, wider road continues on to the village shops and the modern centre of village life.

Ipstones is a particularly interesting place for antiquities. Huge stones abound, and although most of the prominent ones are natural features, they bear tool marks and very early evidence of dwellings built under and alongside them. Hopestone Farm on Park Lane has a fine stone with early tool marks cut into it. At nearby Belmont, there are two huge natural monoliths and, just below the Sharpecliffe end of Ipstones Edge, there are a number of upright stones hiding in a small wood. Some of these also bear evidence of working.

Our line continues down the narrow lane passing between the old and new schools and the Sea Lion public house. Just below the Sea Lion, the lane bears to the left and the line continues through an old blocked up gateway on the right. At this point, a modern footpath allows access to the estate that was built in the orchard behind the present wall. The stone posts are still in situ. You might comment that this is not the first time that our line has departed from the present road for the older track and this is a common feature of our line as it remains true to its origins.

Walk on down the lane and bear to the right and you will see Meadow Place, a fine old yeoman farm building, recently restored. The line emerges down the driveway opposite Well House Farm and crosses the road here. To access the line again, you will need to continue to the main road and turn left. The line is running almost parallel to you through the Industrial Estate and goes behind Paddock Farm into what can still be recognised as a passage between the farm and the adjacent red brick fronted house.

As the main road leaves the village, it curves around the small field in front of the farm and the line can be felt at the edge of the verge by the next gate on the left. If you turn here and look back, you can see the

Stones near Ipstones.

line of the old track quite clearly. The road here is modern and as you would expect, the line passes through another gateway and continues to run alongside the present road for a few hundred yards.

This section of road between Paddock Farm and Hermitage Farm is interesting. Just as the line emerges from the left to join up, the remains of a previous road can be seen rising on the right. All three roads join up by the gate on the right under the line of trees and the line continues to Hermitage Farm. Here it leaves the road again on the right and passes straight down the valley as you might expect. The modern road then twists its way down to Froghall and meets up with the line again just above the point where the canal crosses under the road.

The modern road winds eastwards before joining the A52, while our route drops to the Churnet and crosses at the old ford beneath the road and rail-bridge. As the ancient way now makes its way across country for some distance, we have to take the A521 Churnet Valley Road and turn left into Lockwood Road before picking it up again. You have to pass Thornbury Hall and proceed to the next bend in the road where an arm of Gibridding Wood extends to the road before the line emerges from its cross-country trail across four steep valleys dropping to the Churnet. There are traces of the line as it traverses Highshutt, crosses diagonally over the B5417 and passes through Highshutt Farm towards Lambskin Dale and the Counslow plantation.

Turning left on the B5032, the line emerges from the woods on the left and crosses via a gateway into the field on the right. It follows the field boundary with the Brownbank Plantation and joins an ancient footpath where it establishes itself in its own right once again as a route. This footpath is in a direct line with Sandy Lane down which our line progresses. The junction, a few hundred yards short of the turn for Brown

The line crosses the B 5032.

Bank Farm is interesting as here we find the path marked with large stone gateposts. It marks the division of Sandy Lane into two ancient routes, one for Ipstones along our line and the other via Stoney Dale to Oakamoor.

Looking at Sandy Lane and its footpath extension today, we are reminded of what the track must have looked like in and before medieval times. Without the tarmac it would look little different under its high banks and crowded trees. Just wide enough for a horse drawn wagon, it is cut into the landscape in a straight line for a considerable distance. Just before we get to Lightoaks Farm on the left, and where a private path joins from the right, a leaning mark stone can be seen set at the top of the bank.

Way mark.   Sandy Lane

Quite significant slices of our journey will run along similar straight sections of road. These are mostly found in the open countryside where there has been the least interference with the older patterns of communication. Just above Lightoaks Farm there is a series of ponds fed by a spring and an old well. When we were last there, a heron was enjoying himself fishing.

Passing Lightoaks Farm, there are more ponds fed by the stream that rises below Bradley Elms. Developed and enlarged as medieval fishponds, they are based on an earlier mere. The line here leaves the road and follows the water down the valley before crossing the road at Great Gate at the ford. The position of fords and bridges is always associated with lines and this is no exception.

The Mere fishponds, Sandy Lane.

We are now close to Croxden Abbey and are able to pick up the energies that underpin that religious site. Our line demonstrates quite a different kind of local energy from those

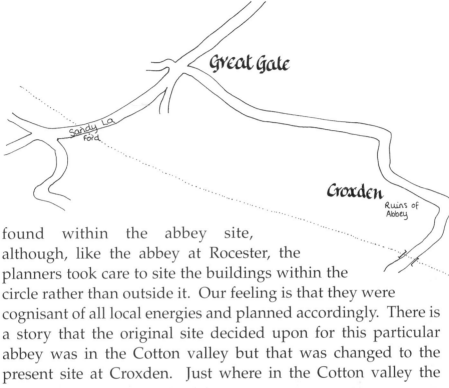

found within the abbey site, although, like the abbey at Rocester, the planners took care to site the buildings within the circle rather than outside it. Our feeling is that they were cognisant of all local energies and planned accordingly. There is a story that the original site decided upon for this particular abbey was in the Cotton valley but that was changed to the present site at Croxden. Just where in the Cotton valley the

The ford at Great Gate.

Croxden Abbey

proposed site was is not known but it is possibly where the present Roman Catholic Church and the sad remains of the school are situated. Certainly the adjacent farm has some extremely old stonework still evident. (Another dowsing exercise for someone!)

The line now leaves the road on the right and after crossing below the quarry, joins the footpath parallel with Croxden Brook. It then crosses the road at the southern end of the bridge over the brook on the road to Abbey View Farm. The modern lane takes a sharp left turn before joining the Roman Road by a pond shortly before Woottons. The line follows the brook for a while before joining the end of a footpath and emerging on to the Roman Road by the milepost at Woottons.

The line now follows the Roman Road into Rocester. There are several energy lines along this important ancient route and our line joins a track-line as it makes for the bridging point over the Churnet. We pass through the town, past the abbey site and Arkwright's mill (1781/2) and on to the second river crossing at the County boundary where the line crosses the Dove. This is an important focal point, the old ford marking the division of territory.

The perimeter now follows the road until the bottom of the drive for Abbotsholme School where it leaves on the left and

Croxden Abbey.

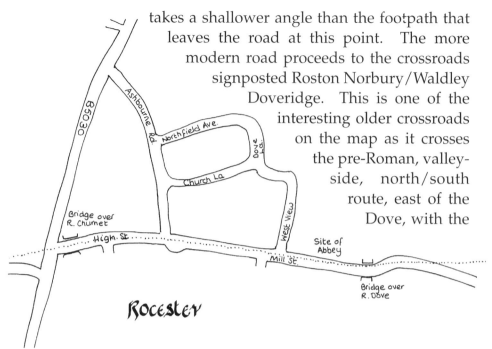

takes a shallower angle than the footpath that leaves the road at this point. The more modern road proceeds to the crossroads signposted Roston Norbury/Waldley Doveridge. This is one of the interesting older crossroads on the map as it crosses the pre-Roman, valley-side, north/south route, east of the Dove, with the

equally ancient pre-Roman track and perimeter line that we are following. Actually the old crossroads lies a hundred yards down Roston Lane where our line crosses the existing road. There are the remains of a pond and overhanging trees in the field on the left. The earlier road from Rocester to Roston goes from Rocester Bridge to Undertown Lane, Roston and today exists as a footpath.

Within half a mile our line joins the road at the junction of two footpaths, one of which has followed the line along a banked field boundary before emerging on the road. Modern road, Roman Road and our line now continue together to Thurvaston crossroads at Springfield Farm and then into Cubley Lane. Just as you pass The Spinney, you can see the symmetrical brickwork of The Howard Arms on the junction of the A515. This is Great Cubley crossroads and the road is now called Derby Lane.

The Mills and the Churnet at Rocester.

The Howard Arms, Great Cubley.

Sometimes the footpath is a little daunting.

Flagshaw Lane. Kirk Langley.

7. Great Cubley to Crossroads Farm, Belper

After passing through Great Cubley the road climbs the eastern side of the Bentley Brook valley and passes on straight towards Bentley Hall on the right. Built in 1613/14 this fascinating building replaced an earlier moated manor house still connected by footpaths to the now vanished medieval village of Hungry Bentley and Bentley Fields Farm. We dowsed the road just outside the Hall and found a complex pattern of energy lines woven together in the centre of the road. The pre-Roman track, the Roman Road, a track line and our perimeter line all travel together along this section. However, within a few hundred yards, they all continue through a gateway and the present road turns abruptly to the left for Alkmonton. This is one of those strange places where, if not alert, the driver is tempted to drive straight on. This is no surprise as natural track lines tend to encourage the animal to stay 'on track' and this is exactly what will happen if the driver follows his natural instincts.

Bentley Hall.

The Roman road and the track lines pass through the gateway ahead.

Our line now continues through a wood and emerges to cross the site of another barrow-mere at Top House Farm. The medieval fishponds here are not on the line. It is not easy to follow this section by modern road as the line tracks along the centre of the old Roman road across the fields. This does not emerge until the junction of Long Lane and Hoargate Lane just south of Ardsley House. Here, four tracks meet on the line. You can actually follow our line along a hundred yards of modern roadway at the junction with Rodsley Lane but it soon leaves the

The line of the Roman Road.

Longford Hall.

road on the left to pass through the grounds of Longford Hall. The large stone on the right of the road is on a track-line and our perimeter line.

The line now hugs the Roman Road behind a band of trees to the left and crosses the Brailsford Brook before joining Long Lane again about half a mile further on. We are now back on the combined system of lines that run straight on to Mackworth, Markeaton and Little Chester. In another two hundred yards you will pass the turning on the right for

Not an original mark - but nevertheless it is on the line.

An ancient well is sited opposite Corner Farm Cottage.

Brookley Meadows Farm. On the left, opposite Corner Farm Cottage, there is a very old spring and well right on the roadside. If you are following the line by motor then this is an easy bit as you pass Stoop Farm crossroads and the settlement of Longlane. Shortly after Longlane there is another ancient crossroads, now a staggered lane/footpath, which develops into Taylors Lane to the south and is marked as Burrows Lane to the north. After crossing Nunsclough Brook and the road to Lees on the right, our line swings into the left-hand ditch and leaves the Roman Road and the older track line a hundred yards before the Kirk Langley turn. We take this turning to the left, and drive over The Green at Langley Green. The line rejoins immediately before the junction with Petty Close Lane from the left. We are now heading for Kirk Langley.

Kirk Langley is another very old site with Saxon remains extant in the church buildings. The line does not follow any of the modern roads but leaves Church Lane on the left a couple of metres before the footpath that drops down to the main Derby/Ashbourne road just short of New House Farm. Our route falls to the right of the footpath until the gateway into the second field, then it swings over to the right again towards the

Kirk Langley

ponds and springs that link to the road's edge. Close to the point where the line leaves Church Lane there are the remains of a shallow pond overhung by a massive willow trunk.

We cannot recommend the stile that joins the A52 by New House Farm. It is lethal; the undergrowth is breast high and the traffic immediate and very close! However, walk back towards the village and the line crosses the main road shortly before the footpath on the left. Thus our line joins the footpath that links to Lodge Lane. To pick it up by car you will need to return to

An old willow trunk overhangs the remains of a pond.   Kirk Langley.

The mere pond in Lodge Lane.

the village and take the turn for Keddleston down Flagshaw Lane. As you turn right into Lodge Lane, our line emerges along the footpath from the left and joins the road again.

The fascinating and validating factor that emerges about this Bronze Age line is the way in which, despite local changes in the domestic landscape, it still shows itself in terms of a continuous broken line. Bits of footpath, lane and farmtrack all line up and answer to the dowsing rod. With a trained eye it becomes visible on the OS map, for example here at Kirk Langley where our line links The Green to Lodge Lane along a system of lanes and muddy paths. Additional confirming evidence comes from the stones and ponds that have weathered the years. Walking these ancient lines, and looking carefully about as you go, makes you realise again and again that the roads, tracks and paths of today owe their origins to the Bronze Age and in some cases, before that.

Our line continues along Lodge Lane, past Lodge Farm and on towards New Park Farm where another mere pond can be seen on the left. The line clips the pond on the verge and then leaves the road through the gate on the right. We take the road

The edge of the mere pond at New Park Farm, Lodge Lane.

as it swings to the left and pick up evidence again as the line passes the mere at the corner where the drive for Meynell Langley House leaves on the right. The line is only evident for a brief yard or two before it crosses the field immediately before the Kedleston Estate and the track for Upper Vicarwood. To follow it now necessitates a visit to the grounds of the house where the line enters through Pleasure Ground Wood.

Dowsing the perimeter as it leaves Lodge Lane

Some meres are almost overgrown and unrecognisable. Crossroads for Meynell Langley.

Sir Nathaniel Curzon (1726-1804), inheriting the estate in 1758, set out to demolish the existing house and to rebuild in a popular contemporary classical style. It was during the early years of the next decade that the grounds were extensively modified, the ancient trees retained as hedges were removed, cottages re-sited and the stream dredged and widened to create a broad pastoral vista. Part of an earlier road to the church was retained as a carriageway from Mercaston Lane end. Old maps

Sheep tracks follow the old road in Kedleston Park.

The line of the old road comes from Pleasure Ground Wood, Keddleston

show that another earlier track crossed this carriageway at the point where it rises to just above 90 metres above sea level at the base of Harepit Hill and led in a north easterly direction to meet the present Kedleston Road. We were able to dowse this quite clearly but not to follow it across the Cutler Brook as there is now no bridge at that point. You might register no surprise to discover that our line followed this older track. We were able to walk almost all of it from Pleasure Ground Wood, across Harepit Hill, across the present carriageway and on down to the water. Perhaps it was not so strange that we discovered a well-worn sheep-track crossing the driveway at almost the spot where the two ancient tracks made a crossroads. We also discovered another very old track crossing our walk, parallel to the present driveway and leading towards The Old Rectory. However, our line and the old trackway continues through Hay Wood, over the road to the sawmills and exits just across from Ireton Farm. If you look at a map you can see that the line of Cumberhills Road towards Duffield is pretty much in a straight line with Lodge Lane on the other side of the estate. This is our line and also an ancient track line.

Cumberhills Road proceeds relatively straight until a swing to the right shortly after Cumberhills Cottages. Now the road deviates from the line and does not rejoin it until almost at the junction with the B5023. It then crosses and can be picked up in Wirksworth Road almost at the junction with Meadow Vale. There is an alleyway at this point and our line follows it, or rather, the alleyway follows the older way. On we go, passing The Meadows Primary School on the left and crossing the River Ecclesbourne. We now follow the line across the Centenary Way footpath and traverse a field to join Holloway Road by the railway line. Crossing the road, there is another footpath running up alongside some beautiful gardens belonging to a large house called The Glen, set off Hazelwood Road below the cemetery. Just by the gates of the large house, the line is strong and dowses well.

Duffield

We are now almost in a straight line with the foot of Cumberhills Road and this is also an ancient track-line. The line takes off across Avenue Road, Chadfield Road and Chevin Road before becoming the footpath that comprises Midshires Way. This footpath continues past Courthouse Farm and enters North Lane.

The footpath from Meadow Vale.   Duffield.

Following by motor, it will now be necessary to return to the Hazelwood Road and make up the hill past the cemetery to the junction with Spring Hollow on the right. Proceed up Firestone Lane to Farnah Green where the line rejoins adjacent to an old stile. We are now in Farnah Green Road heading for the crossroads with the A517.

The gates of The Glen.   Duffield.

Our line is not deterred by road or rail as it sweeps through Duffield.

8. Crossroads Farm, Belper to Newhaven

The staggered crossroads into Dalley Lane comes next and we are on track with the line until Belper Lane End and the Bull's Head public house. All the way up Dalley Lane, the line is dowsable from the passenger side of a motor car. Drive back down and the line has gone! It runs up the left showing us that the original iter was a path only a footpath wide. Turnpiked in 1756, it established itself as a key route from then on. Follow on up Gorses and pass Milnhay and Sandyford Farms on the left. The line stays with the present road until you get to The Smithy opposite Higg Lane. Here the line is right on the middle of the road as we discovered dodging the occasional lorry, which found us wandering back and forth searching for a signal!

The Bull's Head.   Belper Lane End.

This was one of those places where we lost the line altogether. It just seemed to vanish behind a huge nettle bed close to an empty barn at the end of Higg Lane. A little

Higg Lane End.

Windmill Lane.

trespassing in a nearby field found it again heading off across country towards Windmill Lane. Confirmation came in the shape of a classic stone set in the hedge and almost overcome with weeds and grasses. We sat on it and the signal was positive and strong. This was one of those stones that had not moved! Our line now followed Windmill Lane for a hundred yards until it became Pendleton Lane whereupon it left the road on the left. Following the line by car, you can either continue into Alderwasley

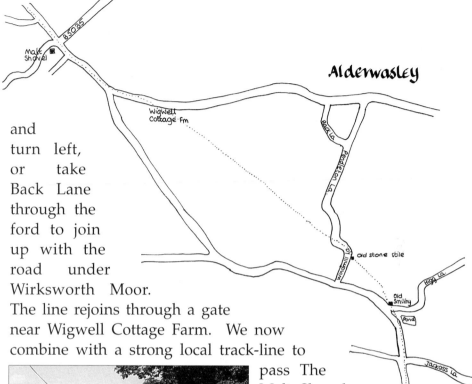

Alderwasley

and turn left, or take Back Lane through the ford to join up with the road under Wirksworth Moor. The line rejoins through a gate near Wigwell Cottage Farm. We now combine with a strong local track-line to

pass The Malt Shovel public house and cross over the B5035.

We are now on the Oakathorpe Road and the line stays with the present road until the footpath on the right at Lantern Cottage. There is a fine old spring here, now lovingly restored.

The footpath swings off to the right but soon returns to the line heading

The line follows the staggered crossroads by the Malt Shovel.

The well at Lantern Cottage.

for Black Rock. At the point where the track turns sharply to the left, the line continues in a straight line for the rock. We can pick it up again in Baker's Lane and on down the footpath to Barnwell Lane. Next comes Bedehouse Lane where the line heads directly for the corner of Scarthin and the large millpond at Cromford.

Cruneford or Crumford speaks of a crooked ford across the river. Sometimes fords do not always pass directly across rivers in the seemingly easiest manner. Where this is the case it is almost certainly because the track-lines do not approach at right angles and make a narrow angle instead. There are many local examples of more modern bridges crossing at variance to the original fords. The bridge at Gypsy Hollow on the edge of Leek is a particularly good example as the ford was paved and much of the original is still in situ. The remains of fords are almost always discernible if you climb down the bank and examine the riverbed.

However, our line does not touch the banks of the Derwent but reaches one of the few angular nodes on its journey. It is strong as it drops down the last few yards of

A footway follows the line down to Cromford from Baker's Lane.

Greyhound Pool.

Cromford Hill and then makes an angle to turn into Scarthin alongside the Greyhound Pool. Water Lane, which develops into the A5012, then takes the line on across Bonsall Hollow, past the Via Gellia Mill and up the Clatterway towards Bonsall. It leaves the main village street on the right via a footpath and then follows a boundary line before emerging alongside The King's Head and the famous cross by the well. Here track-lines and our line meet and the cross is worth dowsing as it marks the spot accurately. It is

Scarthin, Cromford.

The line climbing out of Bonsall.

worth mentioning that although often consisting of a hotch-potch of mixed repairs, most ancient crosses are still more or less in the same place. They were often shifted to accommodate the coming of the motor-car if awkwardly placed but if sufficient fuss was made, local councils were often persuaded to widen the roads around them and poach bits of neighbouring gardens instead. Sometimes the cross, or bits of it, can be found in the walls or hedges nearby but a bit of dowsing will soon establish where it was in the first place.

Our line continues up the High Street to the well at the junction with Pounder Lane. It then clips the corner on the right opposite Abel Lane before continuing up the narrow Bonsall Lane towards Brightgate. This is real limestone country with several redundant 16th and 17th century buildings along the roadside and set in the field corners. Brightgate, like Great Gate, denotes an ancient way and the perimeter line passes through what was once a much larger community. Next along Bonsall Lane comes Blakelow Farm under Blakelow Hill and we continue past Bonsall Lane Farm to the junction with the

The line crosses a farm track as a depression.

Grangemill to Winster road. Here the line carries straight on but we must take a right turn, then a swift left and another left to join the road for Newhaven. An interesting point here is that, as the line crosses a farm track off the Newhaven road, it can be seen as a depression in the track nearly always filled with water. At this complex junction of ways the Saxon Portway strikes through on its way north crossing the Newhaven road from the Grangemill direction. The line connects again within two hundred yards and runs straight for a mile or two under another Blake Low at 330 metres and a limestone reef on the right.

Our line here joins a track-line and the two merge to form a strong foundation for the Pikehall to Winster road. At the bottom of the hill just before you enter Pikehall, the line leaves the tarmac and sweeps away to the right to clip the near end of the line of trees that extend to Pike Hall Farm. As the A5012 climbs up the bank towards Newhaven Crossing (High Peak Trail) the road can be seen to swing to the left. Our line rejoins here from the right and continues along the tarmac to the junction with the Friden road.

Pikehall.

The line at Newhaven as it leaves the road by the Friden turn.

9. Newhaven to Bottomhouse

This is one of those interesting situations where the eye can plainly see how the old road and naturally, our line, continues on a straight course behind the garage whilst we have to sweep round to the left before joining the Ashbourne to Buxton highway. We now turn right and find the line coming through the trees on our right and crossing the main road over a wall by the side of a small wood. The animal track here is so strong that the wall is consistently broken down at the point where our line crosses.

The line then rises to 368 metres before passing close to End Low and entering the remains of a fascinating and seldom used walled limestone drift-way that cannot have changed much in a thousand years. This is still our road and indeed it was a road in ancient times. I can think of no better example of what a Bronze Age track must have looked like. Eruptions of the same limestone reef we noted earlier can be seen on the right as it forms the northern barrier to our circle. If the reader wishes to step back in time then this is the place.

A step back in time - an ancient way.

Following the line across to End Low.

The track now develops into a rough roadway and joins the Heathcote to Newhaven Cottage road by the remains of a pond. We turn left and head downhill towards Heathcote. The line tracks alongside on the left between limestone walls and although mainly tree-filled is easily discernible as an old road. In fact it is an old limestone causeway and the great flags can still be seen lying haphazardly along the way. This present section of current roadway was constructed to facilitate

The old roadway runs alongside.

Thickly turfed in winter but overgrown in summer, the drift
carries the line into Heathcote.

bridging the railway line. Our perimeter line soon rejoins the modern roadway close to the stone walled roundabout and then drops down just inside the grounds of Heathcote Hall Farm to a cleft sighting stone set just over the right hand wall under a tree. Our line then continues alongside the present road to Heathcote Mere where five tracks meet. This is a classical example of an old route mere-pond where two major lines cross. Here

The sighting stone at Heathcote Hall Farm.

we have the Long Dale, Biggin Dale and Dove Dale track crossing our circle line. The mere is fed by a spring and there is also an old well. The name of the road that leads towards Hartington is called High Cross which suggests that there might have existed a mark at this point as well as a mere.

Our line is strong here and leads us up the hill towards the village of Hartington. Just at the

A515

B5054

Hartington

Heathcote

Newhaven

Well

High Cross

Heathcote
Mere

The Old
Mill
Mill La.

Bridge over
R. Dove

The animals still follow the line.

brow of the hill there is another classic way-stone currently acting as a gatepost. It is far larger than the other gate pillars on the road and although having two bar or rope holes, it dwarfs its companions and stands out for what it is. Moreover it is visible from the sighting stone at Heathcote Hall Farm and marks the route across the mere and up the hill on the other side. The line now drops down Hall Bank past Hartington Hall.

This particular area is fascinating. Just to the north of Heathcote is the most southerly Viking burial yet discovered. The mere was, according to local tradition, maintained by monks from Nottinghamshire who made a charge for watering stock. This implied monastic ownership is in keeping with its ancient origins and importance. There is also a tradition that the area was feared by the old drovers as

The large way-mark looking towards Hall Bank.

lawless and cattle-rustling country.

Just to the south there are some classic examples of packhorse tracks, complete with their giant way-stones and enclosure walls. The name High Cross (as in other places - compare High Cross at the junction of Watling Street and the Fosse Way) invokes the one time presence of a significant way mark, and this prompted us to dowse the area to see just where this might have been. Our first search was on the high ground close to the parish boundary line above Heathcote Mere on the Hartington side. Although we discovered that a cross did once stand here it was not too be seen.

Finding the cross or remains of it, and just where it originally stood engaged our curiosity for some time. Eventually after much walking and dowsing we established that the original site was on the first cross roads south-east from Hartington on the packhorse route below Brighton. It had subsequently been moved to High Cross Lane where the name had stuck.

The remains of it were not far away! Currently acting as a gate post, it can be found above Harding's Gap, at the end of Harding's Lane, in a field called Underhills. It was not hard to find as it

The remains of High Cross.

Heathcote Mere.

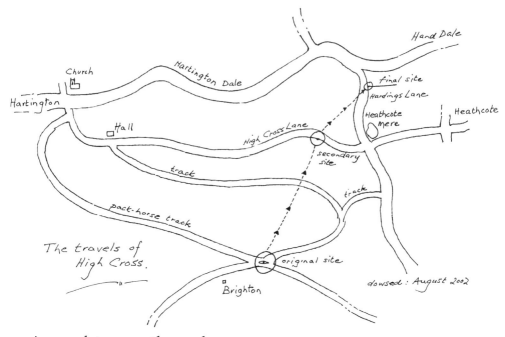

is sandstone - the only piece of sandstone in a forest of limestone. It also carried two iron straps to bind a line of weakness - thus confirming its importance. What remains is only a portion, the strengthened centre section of a large and geographically errant structure. The imported sandstone would have stood out as a vibrant mark in the limestone area. It was firstly an important mark, it was then moved and took its name with it, and it has

Iron straps fix the old cross shaft

now found an ignominious end as a post a third of a mile from its first site. Somewhere the sandstone base, or parts of it, will be languishing, perhaps already in some field boundary.

At the bottom of the hill, on the outskirts of Hartington, the road swings to the right but we were able to follow the line through a gate on the left. It does not follow through the adjacent stile and along the footpath as you might expect, but tracks through the garden of Reynards Close and emerges by the side of an old well in the field a few yards to the left of the footpath as it skirts the garden boundary. This is a case of a present property causing a slight deviation in the old footpath that was following the line. Within a few more yards the line rejoins the footpath to pass through a stile built from two giant slabs of limestone. This stile is still in its original place and the line passes through the centre. Another case of the original stones being still in situ. On limestone land, pretty well all the original marks are made from huge hewn chunks of limestone, and the dressed grit-stone gateposts and stiles easily stand out and are seen to be 17th century imports.

You will now need to squeeze through a wall and join another track that emerges to the left of the Pottery. The line however, passes to the right of the Pottery through a jungle of nettles and brambles. You can see the way of it despite it not being a current right of way.

Although Hartington presents much as an 18th century village it is a great deal older and the church has fragments of pre-conquest carved stonework incorporated into its fabric. Possibly the oldest is a small Saxon stone in the wall of the north transept. St. Giles church stands elevated just outside our perimeter but has its own scheme of energy lines that underpin its position. By an amazing stroke of luck the spring that emerges from under the churchyard is still evident and can be seen by the steps that lead to the south door. So rare to see a holy site with its spring still in working order.

Hartington.

Hartington Hall.

Our line comes from Reynards Close and passes through these
marks before heading for Hartington Bridge.

Cross over Mill Lane and you will see a small footpath
that passes down the side of a building. This too is tight and
there are plenty of nettles nicely knee high, so watch out! Our
line passes this way and makes for The Mill House at
Hartington Bridge. This is an interesting bridge as there are
remains of previous crossings but our line crosses diagonally
from the line of the footpath on the right to the very end of the
bridge on the left. Worked stones below the present
Staffordshire bank suggest that the original ford followed
likewise.

Our line now climbs from the water and passes across the
field to the left of the road. It rejoins the road just past Raikes
Farm on the bend by the driveway to Beresford Cottage. We are
now heading for Hulme End (Old Norse for water meadow)
and the line is with the road until we get to Bank House Farm.
Here the line passes over the Manifold to the north of the
present bridge and crosses the field to exit on the main road by
Manifold House. This field is interesting as it contains evidence
of the river's old course as it meandered through the water

Hartington Bridge over the Dove.

Hulme End Bridge.

meadow. The present road, developed from the turnpike, is raised on a causeway as it crosses the meadow between the bank at Bank House Farm and the opposite bank behind Manifold House. Although there is evidence of a ford north of the bridge, the old ford must have been in the water meadow close to our line. We have not dowsed in the field but the ancient crossing should be apparent to any dowser.

Before we get to Cowlow House and the junction with Cowlow Lane, the line again leaves the road by the entrance to the car-park on the left and runs up the hill just wide of Cowlow Barn. There is evidence of an old bridge or stepping stone across the Hayes Brook close by and there is also a stone set in the field which provides a sight up the hill. Just on the north side of the turnpike is a spring. The line rejoins Cowlow Lane just above Copse Field Cottage and passes Cliff House and Dale Cottage on its way towards the end of Butts Lane. It swings behind Hobcraft Farm and we pick it up again strongly on the tarmac as it follows the B5053 through Warslow towards Shay Side.

Crossing the Manifold at Hulme End. Manifold House,
which the line passes, is visible in the background.

Cowlow Lane.

Warslow is interesting as our line crosses a strong energy line on the road close to the church and school. It emerges from the left, marked by a stone stile and passes through the yew in the churchyard. Dowsing established that the old cross base presently reclining against the church wall once stood here, some three feet from the stile and in the present road. It was likely moved when the turnpike was built and the track widened.

Our line leaves the road again for a short distance to pass to the left of Shay Side Farm and picks up just short of Brownlow Farm. We cross the Warlslow Brook at Brownlow Bridge and the line is firmly in the centre of the road. If you look over the bridge on the right you can see the remains of the old ford under a tree. It is highly likely that the original ford was under the bridge on our line, the secondary ford was this one to the right and the present bridge built when the turnpike was established in stone. The ground here is swampy and wall-plates and tie-bars indicate that the bridge has shifted. In fact you can see this for yourself if you observe the courses of the stones as they leave the horizontal on the north side.

As the B5053 now snakes up the hill, our line does the direct thing - as it did at Froghall - and reaches for the ridge via a standing stone in the field to the right as you climb. The line joins the road

Warslow Cross base..

The mark for the low at Warslow.

Brownlow Bridge.

Brownlow Ford.

again at the crest of the hill at the big bend by the driveway to
Hill Farm. You can stand by the stone wall at the drive's end
and see Warslow church in a direct line with the standing stone.
We reckon that the cross at Warslow would have lined up well.

Brownlow Hill.

Our line is strong again across Butterton Moor, passing the turn
for Grindon Moor known for the story of the Headless
Horseman. It is stories like these that anchor these old tracks
firmly in the Celtic era. Any reference to the severed head is a
reminder of the cult of head worship. To associate this with the
horse is doubly significant as the horse was also sacred to the
Celts. It is very likely that this particular variation of the story
was established to protect the many lows that are to be found
across Grindon Moor and the surrounding area. One of note is
the low that has been planted with a single tree shortly before
you get to the crossroads for Butterton. This was dug within
recent times and confirmed as a Bronze Age round-barrow with
funerary remains.

We now drop down the bank towards the village of

The site of the old church at Onecote.

Onecote, past the site of the old church on the left in the angle of land that lies between the road and Titterton Lane. Next comes the old ford and present bridge across the still youthful Hamps as it flows on towards the hamlet of Ford. Our line is then to be found pretty well in the middle of the road as it strikes up the hill past New Farm and Pewit Hall Farm on the left. At 373 metres it crosses the ancient moor ridge-way known as Morridge and begins its descent to the Green Man at Bottomhouse. Look out on the left shortly before Newhouse Farm and you will see the remains of a stone circle that has been dragged out of the field and piled in a corner. The stones were sited stones but are no longer in their rightful place. A few hundred yards down towards Hobmeadows Farm there is another standing stone and indications that there was another circle in the vicinity. Possible remnants of this are to be found in a small copse to the rear of the farm.

We are now back to Bottomhouse, where we started out on our journey.

Barrows set with trees which now emphasise their sites.

Conclusions

We do not think for one minute that this dowsed perimeter line is unique. There must be thousands of similar patterns of energy around our country. Guy Underwood has amply demonstrated that track-lines of energy underpin most ancient roadways and that these roadways are the basis of the modern network we see around us every day. There are also several recently discovered vast landscaped Zodiacal figures sculpted into the landscape which have stimulated much speculation as to their extent.

What we have been following is, however, not a simple track-line or part of a figurative relief but a water related line that is found for most of the way closely related to local track-lines. Where they are present together, they often run side by side or overlap. It sometimes becomes complex as on the approach to Rocester and outside Bentley Hall, when there are a number of dowsable lines in association with each other. Being a water related line has meant that there are perhaps a more than average number of meres on our journey, the most remarkable being Heathcote Mere which lies on limestone.

Underpinning all we have been following is the basic premise that all old roads, tracks and paths are where they are because of the patterns of energy found in the earth below them. This is why the Druids were able to arbitrate so easily in the matter of a moved boundary. They simply dowsed and the answer was plain. If the stone had been moved by an unscrupulous neighbour, the Druids could put it back on the line in a matter of minutes just as we can discover the site of an old stile if it has been moved to accommodate a new housing development.

Most earth energy lines answer to the presence of underlying geological features, faults, stresses, heavy mineralisation and the like. Some are found on a national basis and some are quite local. What our Bronze Age ancestors felt they had discovered was a means whereby the earth was

nick - sight...

revealing itself in terms of power. Similarly they recognised that the phases of the moon affected planting and the tides. No more than a sensitivity to their environment really. What developed from this was that certain lines of energy supported animals and humans whilst others had a detrimental effect. This is still very true although we disregard it nowadays and suffer the consequences.

Thus we find healing and balancing resonances along the lines that underpin our churches and busy excitable lines on old market-cross sites. Our line appears to add something to the locality and bring in an additional factor that amplifies what is found at the centre. Certainly there is a measurable difference inside the circle and this must have been the reason for its inception.

There have been a number of critics telling us that this amazing circle is just a chance formation, a haphazard pattern of roads that merely appear to fit into a circle. In fact we looked initially at a number of possible circumnavigations that made a better and more regular circle than the one we ended up with. We had to be entirely objective and react to the rod rather than force our way around a far smoother route. What we ended up with was the flattened ellipse we describe. It is not tidy. In fact it wriggles and wobbles here and there as it sweeps around on its course. What became for us incontrovertible proof of the whole were the marks and meres, stiles and posts, tracks and

Way mark ...

paths, gates and hedge-lines that were still in situ after so many hundreds of years. Also the fact that much of the way was still visible from points of high ground as the line could be seen leading through a gateway at just the point where the current road deviates. After a while it all became too much of a coincidence to be anything else but deliberate.

Although its original purpose might have been to outline an area of the countryside that was conducive to calm and healing, its bounds, recognised also by the animal kingdom in terms of their many concentrated tracks, were walked, delineated and marked. These in turn became the original walkways and patterns of local communication. As with all things, the proof of the pudding lies in the eating and we invite anyone to sample the difference for themselves. The spring is still active beneath Ashbourne church despite thousands of gallons being drawn off each day. The line still runs up the centre, although a little to the north today, and there is still a powerful healing spot upon the line for those who wish to avail themselves of it. There are resurgences of energy at the edge of the churchyard and again just short of the roundabout on the Mayfield Road and of course, there is the outer perimeter that we have been following in these pages.

Just what enables us as humans to draw up energies from

the earth is still not known. Our own theory is that there is more of an affinity between the molecules of earth and those constituting our bodies than is realised. We are, after all, of the earth, as are all living creatures and plants. It is then perhaps not surprising that agitations or vibrations on a particle or sub-molecular level can be appreciated. Dowsing is perhaps no more than sensitivity to particle energy and the greater picture beneath our feet that our distant ancestors became aware of.

Lastly, whether we appreciate it or not, we are the beneficiaries of a vast knitted folk pattern, the warp and weft of deliberate comings and goings in our land for thousands of years. This crumpled net, although much patched, is still as potent a part of the living landscape as the lows themselves, high landscape icons, still visible as intended and trailing power across the millennia. Dowsing only sharpens the ability to recognise it.

Simple Steps for the Beginner

Using the rod

Seeing someone with a dowsing rod or a forked stick always arouses interest. We know that from our many outings into the countryside when folk come up and say, "Are you water divining?"

Sometimes it will be a water board man who is using the quick way to find the main or it might be a local farmer searching for his land drains. Whatever the quest, the dowser promotes curiosity. We have heard all the usual questions and are always careful to explain just what we are up to. So, if you have found this little book interesting you might like to try some dowsing for yourself.

To begin with you will need an instrument. The most common and the one usually recommended for beginners, is the humble metal coat hanger. Cut it and bend it into a right angle. Size is not an issue as long as the handle extends the width of your palm and the arm reaches out far enough to see it move. You do not need two; one is quite satisfactory. If a coat hanger is a problem, a length of brazing wire or galvanised wire will do equally well.

Grasp the handle loosely to allow the handle the freedom to swivel within your hand. A common fault is to hold the instrument too tightly. This will prevent the arm from moving. You can slip the handle into some sort of sleeve if you wish. A spent biro case or a plastic drinking straw will do admirably. This allows the arm to rotate freely but it also requires a little more care in balancing. Next, line up the instrument's arm with your forearm. It helps if you tilt the arm very slightly downwards as this puts a little tension into the operation.

Practice handling and balancing the instrument a few times as above. Now you are ready for action.

Metal rods have been in use since the early 17th century and there is a record that the famous dowser Martine de Bertereau used metal rods from 1602 to 1645. However, if you wish to be entirely traditional, you may like to fashion a rod from hazel. Abbe de Vallemont in 1693 thus described the hazel rod:

'A forked branch of hazel, a foot and a half long, as thick as the finger and if possible, not more than a year old.'

In a publication of 1809, we find another description:

'It must consist of two branches of equal size and of the same length, taken from shoots at the top of the tree. It should be cut below the knot, so as to form a fork and the leaves should be stripped.'

Obviously the rod needs to be sufficiently supple for the ends to be bent almost at right angles. The rod is then held in both hands, palms uppermost with the shaft extending in front of you. Movement of the stem will indicate you are over whatever you are asking for.

Next we need something to dowse; something to activate your response. Water is probably the most simple and there is certainly plenty of it about. A water pipe will enter every home so there is the first exercise you might like to try. Alternatively, a water main will likely travel along most roads and will generate a far stronger signal. Moving water is better as it is the tumbling molecules that produce the energy. To get a response you will need to walk over the area where you suspect the main to be.

However, and this is the nub of it all, you will need to tune in or concentrate solely on what you expect to find. Everything else must be excluded from your mind. It must be a totally dedicated, single-minded operation. If you like, create a mental picture of the flowing stream, swirling in the darkness below your feet. Ask for it. Seek it. Now it is time to start that slow walk, holding the instrument lightly and balanced as we have told you. Try it again, and if not successful, again.

The first indication will be a slight (and it can be very slight) movement of the arm to the right or the left. Either is OK. Failure is usually due to concentrating on the holding of the rod rather than what you are looking for. Remember, it is not a magic instrument, it is you that are dowsing and the instrument only enlarges your response so that you become aware of it more easily. If you got a twitch, then you are on the way to becoming a dowser.

Using the pendulum

Not everyone feels at home with a dowsing rod and some folk find it very hard work. So if the rod is not for you there is an alternative. This is the pendulum, an instrument that has been in use for thousands of years. Perhaps because it so simple it was the tool used more readily by the countrywoman for swift answers. The one that comes to mind is the sexing of newly hatched chickens using a wedding ring on the end of a piece of cotton. Another was to discover the sex of an unborn child or whether the lady was with child in the first place. All very simple stuff for the wise woman. A more serious use was to determine which particular herb was the most relevant to a condition.

How is this done? Well, it is not just a case of waving a ring over a person and expecting the ring to do something magic. There is more to it than that. Firstly we need a simple instrument and this, as we have shown, only needs to be a weight on the end of a piece of cotton or string so that it may rotate freely. You might have seen all sorts of dowsing pendulums and there are those who tell you that what is hanging on the end matters. We have seen everything from polished rock crystal to expensive semi-precious stones but in truth, it matters more whether the thing is comfortable to use and works for you. When you have mastered it, then you can get a fancy one but to begin with, find a small weight and fix it to a length of twine or cotton. A bead or a small lead fishing weight will do.

Next it is important to discover what sort of a response you will get when you try to use it. To hold the instrument so that you may obtain the maximum results you will need to suspend the cotton over the top of the second joint of your forefinger and grasp it with your thumb thus allowing two or three inches to dangle free. The length is critical, as too long a line will result in a very slow action. Now set the pendulum swinging to and fro in line with your thumb. A gentle motion of the wrist should suffice to get a nice rhythm going.

Like the rod, you will need to observe a response so you will have to distinguish between a positive and a negative answer. Now, some folk generate a clockwise movement and others, an anti-clockwise but it matters little as either can be taken as your personal signal to affirm the positive. A question that you might ask is, "What is my yes?" as you set your pendulum in motion. This should give you your physical response in terms of a circling instead of a back and forth motion. Once generated, this will become your permanent positive response to your questions.

Go back to the water main and try crossing and re-crossing it, asking as before for an indication of water. As you go, set the pendulum gently swinging to and fro. As you cross the water you should develop your personal reaction. For us it is an anti-clockwise movement and as quick as the rod. You can always check that you are receptive by asking for your personal yes before walking.

Your negative can be the opposite of your positive reaction or you can allocate a lack of any reaction to the negative and reserve the opposite swing as a maybe. This sounds complicated but it is really a logical set of guides that will soon become second nature.

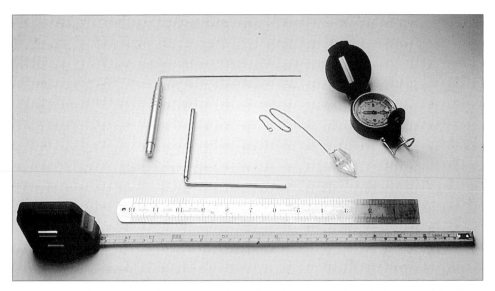

Once you have mastered this or at least been able to obtain a clear yes, you will be able to take the use of the pendulum into a wider field of use. Perhaps the most useful is to use it in conjunction with a pointer. Let me explain.

Let us say, for example, that we have a list of several hundred people who might be helpful in a particular situation. We need to reduce them to an expert few that might be of vital use. Using a pointer, perhaps a pencil in this case, in the left hand; take the pendulum in the right hand and proceed to scan the list. Remember to have the question firmly in your mind as you go and you should find the pendulum reacting to that charismatic few who are able to be of particular value. Try it with the telephone book when you really need someone, but do not panic, and remember to keep that question in mind.

Scanning the wider scene you will need a pointer and a map. This will open up the world of map-dowsing wherein you will be able to locate your objective and cut down on the time you might otherwise have taken tracking back and forth in the field. We shall cover this aspect of dowsing again when we talk about some of the more practical aspects of dowsing.

Practicalities and uses

Once you have the initial skills in hand, the rod and pendulum will become valuable tools in the search for both knowledge and understanding of elements outside your immediate sensory experience.

You have been asked by a farmer to locate his field drainage system. Walking over the land you find indications of water in several places. Making sense of these is so much easier if your rod could indicate direction and thus reveal the flow of a particular stream. With dowsing this is possible. When you get a positive reaction over a water source simply stand and ask for the direction of the flow. Your rod should swing in the appropriate direction. Next, command your rod to follow and simply walk after it. You can blend the action into one operation. Ask for the water and hold the flow in mind. You should then be able to walk along the pipe. Then check out the next pipe in the series. Remember that it is easier to follow moving water, so dowsing after rain is preferable.

You have been asked to find a well in a field that has long been abandoned and filled up with rubbish. You can do this with a preliminary map-dowse or by walking the field edges and asking for bearings. Map-dowsing entails drawing a sketch map of the field, or better, obtaining the relevant OS (1:25,000 scale) map and asking for bearings from the north and east sides of the area in question. These bearings can be drawn on the paper thus providing the co-ordinates to the site you seek. You can then go to the field and search in the orthodox way in a much smaller area than you would do without the map.

Alternatively, if you feel like some exercise, walk the field boundary on the northern side and ask for an indication when you are opposite the well. When your rod reacts, tie a handkerchief in the hedge. Next, walk the eastern edge of the field and do likewise. Then walk out into the field until opposite your marker and you will be in the vicinity of the old well. Dowse for a spring or water source. You can dowse to ask whether the source is potable and also the depth the farmer will need to go down to. Depth is almost always approximate as different strata modify the dowsing signal. However it will be accurate enough to work to and usually within a metre or so.

The method of discerning depth is called the Bishop's rule, after the Bishop of Grenoble. It goes like this. From the location site, walk away from the point and ask for an indication when you are as far from it as the water is below. Then measure your walk.

Remember, a pendulum is equally as good an instrument for all these undertakings and will indicate direction by swinging along the detected flow.

Much of this book has been dealing with following a perimeter line and detecting the boundary between a field of energy and the lack of it. This has necessitated tuning in to the field and becoming used to walking in and out of it. It became very much an automatic reaction as we dowsed hundreds of times on hundreds of locations but always for the same resonant frequency. The simple way was just to ask when we crossed over and to mark the spot. As far as we know there is no generic term in dowsing terminology for such a pool of energy except to say that it is definitely related to water rather than earth energy.

Underhill, in his book, talks of earth energy lines as 'geodetic' lines and most dowsers are aware that they can detect and identify a range of earth energy lines of various dimensions and complexities. We are familiar with most of them. To ascertain whether or not a particular roadway or ancient building is situated upon an earth energy line you only need to walk the ground and ask. Similarly, water lines are also easily identifiable.

Soon you will be able to discover for yourself that the roads and tracks we have been following across the counties of Derbyshire and Staffordshire are based on energy lines. A simple road, if old enough, will lie over lines and will be crossed by lines. Roman roads are interesting to dowse as you can ask if there was an earlier road underneath. Then whether or not there is a central energy line or an associated line. We found that for much of our circle, it coincided with local energy lines thus making it a curiosity in its own right and establishing a premise for its foundation.

Dowsing the landscape is only one of the many aspects of the art. You will find after a while that the limits extend to the breadth of your personal curiosity. You will also discover that dowsing will lead you into the area you are best able to develop and you will become well versed in a particular discipline. Starting to dowse and adapting to the single minded, unambiguous and logical questioning necessary for sensible answers needs intelligence and sensitivity. We have only touched on some of the basic aspects here but are very willing to share our knowledge with the genuinely curious and adventurous who may like to venture on the wider seas of available data under their feet and beyond.

There are a number of introductory books available in the bookshops and they are all good and well able to guide the beginner into the fundamentals of this subject. In the end there is no substitute for practice as much of dowsing becomes peculiar to the individual dowser. This is a subject where you can make up you own rules, systems and schemes and your rod will work accordingly. You will find that there is any number of right ways to tackle some of the skills but the fact is that your own way, if developed sufficiently carefully, will be the equal of any of them. No two advanced dowsers will work in exactly the same way but their results will tally very closely. There is a great deal to learn and even the most skilled dowser will admit that he or she is not at the end of it by any means. There are always surprises.

We wish you the best of luck with your efforts, but then, as you will learn, it is not luck that guides but intuition, the other word for natural dowsing.

Standing on the line inside Longford Yew.

The End